T0194938

LEET Talk

LEET Talk

EDWORDOW COLAGROSSI

Rev. date: 06/12/2020

To order additional copies of this book, contact:
Xlibris
AU TFN: 1 800 844 927 (Toll Free inside Australia)
AU Local: 0283 108 187 (+61 2 8310 8187 from outside Australia)
www.Xlibris.com.au
Orders@Xlibris.com.au
788776

You may have a need, you may not, or you may just want to know how to secure text in its most easiest form with out the use of having to be a cryptographer but still wanting to be cryptologic with your text.

A difference between CODE and CIPHER.

What this book wishes to demonstrate, is really CODE rather than a pure CIPHER.

This is a basic form of CODE which can be seen as acting as a deterrent to anyone looking on who is unfamiliar with the coded characters, numbers and letters.

It may be a Facebook update, it could be an entire book or novel, what ever the cause for the CODE, let it be!

It does not matter if it is small or CAPS the text to be coded, as the code is applied for both sizes of text irrespective of if it is small or CAPS.

THIS CODE IS FOR THE ENGLISH ALPHABET ONLY!

This book wishes to teach you how to LEET TALK or 1337 741K

OR IN CODE SEE BELOW

Y0u w4y h4Ae 4 z33d, y0u w4y z07, 02 y0u w4y ju57 m4z7 70 kz0m h0m 70 53cu23 73x7 1z 175 w05t 3451357 f02w m175 0u7 7h3 u53 0f h4v1zg 70 63 4 c2y9706249h32 8u7 571ll m4z71zg 70 b3 c2y9701061c m17h y0u2 73x7.

4 d1ff323zc3 837m33z C0D3 and C19H32. Mh47 7h15 800k m15h35 70 d3w0z572473, 15 23411y C0D3 247h32 7h4z 4 9u23 C19H32.

7h15 15 4 8451c f02w 0f C0D3 mh1ch c4z 83 533z 45 4c71n6 45 4 d3773223z7 70 4zy0z3 l00k1n6 0z mh0 15 uzf4w17142 m17h ch424c7325, zuw8325 4zd 73tt325.

17 w4y 83 4 f4c3800k u9d473, 17 c0u7d 83 4z 3z7123 800k 02 z0v37, mh4t3a32 7h3 c4u53 f02 7h3 C0D3, 73t 17 83!

17 d035 z07 w47732 1f 1t 1s 5w477 02 C495 7h3 73x7 70 63 c0d3d, 45 7h3 c0d3 15 499713d f02 807h 51N35 0f 7h3 73x7 1223593c71v3 0f 1f 17 15 5w477 or C49s.

7h15 c0d3 15 f02 7h3 3z6715h 47ph4837 0Z7Y!

Introduction

You may have a need, you may not, or you may just want to know how to secure text in its most easiest form with out the use of having to be a cryptographer but still wanting to be cryptologic with your text.

A difference between CODE and CIPHER.

What this book wishes to demonstrate, is really CODE rather than a pure CIPHER.

This is a basic form of CODE which can be seen as acting as a deterrent to anyone looking on who is unfamiliar with the coded characters, numbers and letters.

It may be a Facebook, Twitter, update, it could be an entire book or novel, what ever the cause for the CODE, let it be!

It does not matter if it is small or CAPS the text to be coded, as the code is applied for both sizes of text irrespective of if it is small or CAPS.

THIS CODE IS FOR THE ENGLISH ALPHABET ONLY!

CODE ON NEXT PAGE.

Introduction

Y0u w4y h4Ae 4 z33d, y0u w4y z07, 02 y0u w4y ju57 m4z7 70 kz0m h0m 70 53cu23 73x7 1z 175 w05t 3451357 f02w m175 0u7 7h3 u53 0f h4vlzg 70 63 4 c2y9706249h32 8u7 571ll m4z71zg 70 b3 c2y9701061c m17h y0u2 73x7.

4 d1ff323zc3 837m33z C0D3 and C19H32. Mh47 7h15 800k m15h35 70 d3w0z572473, 15 23411y C0D3 247h32 7h4z 4 9u23 C19H32.

7h15 15 4 8451c f02w 0f C0D3 mh1ch c4z 83 533z 45 4c71n6 45 4 d3773223z7 70 4zy0z3 l00k1n6 0z mh0 15 uzf4w17142 m17h ch424c7325, zuw8325 4zd 73tt325.

17 w4y 83 4 f4c3800k u9d473, 17 c0u7d 83 4z 3z7123 800k 02 z0v37, mh4t3a32 7h3 c4u53 f02 7h3 C0D3, 73t 17 83!

17 d035 z07 w47732 1f 1t 1s 5w477 02 C495 7h3 73x7 70 63 c0d3d, 45 7h3 c0d3 15 499713d f02 807h 51N35 0f 7h3 73x7 1223593c71v3 0f 1f 17 15 5w477 or C49s.

7h15 c0d3 15 f02 7h3 3z6715h 47ph4837 0Z7Y!

A

The letter A.
The first vowel, and first letter of the English modern alphabet.

It can be written as follows in 1337 C0D3;
A = 4 OR V

Examples of A in C0D3:
Aries = 4RIES OR 42135 Ape = 4pe OR 493
Area = 4rea OR 4234

B

The letter B.
The second letter of the English modern alphabet.

It can be written as follows in 1337 C0D3;

B = 8 OR 6

Examples of B in C0D3:

Bart = 8art OR 8427
Bass = 8a55 OR 8455
Bomb = 6om6 or 80w.8

C

The letter C.
The third letter of the English modern alphabet.

In 1337 code no such code exists for masking the letter c. A usual letter C applies amongst code.

Examples of C in C0D3:

Code = C0d3
Cobweb = C06m36
Coca Cola = C0c4 C074

D

The letter D.
The fourth letter of the English modern alphabet.

In 1337 code no such code exists for masking the letter d. A usual letter D applies amongst other letters or code.

Examples of D in C0D3:

Detonate = D370z473
Dominate = D0w1z473
Daylight = D4y716h7

E

The letter E.
The second vowel, and fifth letter of the English modern alphabet.

It can be written as follows in 1337 C0D3;
E = 3

Examples of E in C0D3:

Enter = 3nt3r OR 3z732 Ensure = 3nsur3 or 3z5u23
Entity = 3nt1ty or 3z717y

F

The letter F.
The sixth letter of the English modern alphabet.

In 1337 code no such code exists for masking the letter d. A usual letter D applies amongst other letters or code.

Examples of F in C0D3:

Fish = Fi5h OR F15h Front = F2ont OR f20z7
Family = F4mily OR f4w17y

G

The letter G.
The seventh letter of English modern alphabet.

It can be writen as follows in 1337 C0D3:
G = 6 SOMETIMES 9

Examples of G in C0D3:

Goat = 6oat OR 9047
Gamer = 6amer OR 64w32
Gong = 6ong OR 60z9

H

The letter H.
The eight letter of the English modern alphabet.

In 1337 code no such code exists for masking the letter h. A usual letter H applies amongst other letters or code.

Examples of H in C0D3:

Home = h0me OR h0w3
House = h0use OR h0u53
Hotel = h0tel OR h0731

I

The letter I.
The third vowel and ninth letter of the English modern alphabet.

It can be writen as follows in 1337 C0D3:
I = 1

Examples of I in C0D3:

High = H1gh OR H19h
India = 1nd1a OR 1zd14
Ice = 1ce OR 1c3

J

The letter J.
The tenth letter of the English modern alphabet.

In 1337 code no such code exists for masking the letter j. A usual letter J applies amongst other letters or code.

Examples of J in C0D3:

John = J0hn OR J0hz
Janitor = J4nitor OR J4z1702
Jam = J4m OR J4w

K

The letter K.
The eleventh letter of the English modern alphabet.

In 1337 code no such code exists for masking the letter k. A usual letter K applies amongst other letters or code.

Examples of K in C0D3:

King Kong = K1ng Kong or K1z9 K0z9
Kindle = K1ndle or K1zd73
Kitten = K1tten or K1773z

L

The letter L.
The twelfth letter of the English modern alphabet.

It can be written as follows in 1337 C0D3;
L = 1 OR 7

Examples of L in C0D3:

Lord = 1ord or 102d
Larry = 7arry or 7422y
Lemming = 7emming or 73ww1z9

M

The letter M.
The thirteenth letter of the English modern alphabet.

It can be written as follows in 1337 C0D3;
M = W

Examples of M in C0D3
:
More = Wore OR W023
Merry = Werry OR W322y
Monk = Wonk OR W0zk

N

The letter N.
The fourteenth letter of the English modern alphabet.

It can be written as follows in 1337 C0D3:
N = z

Examples of N in COD3:

Nelly = Zelly or Z377y
Number = Zumber or Zuw832
Nice = Zice or Z1c3

O

The letter O.
The fourth vowel and fifteenth letter in the English modern alphabet.

It can be written as follows in C0D3:
O = 0 (zero)

Examples of O in C0D3:

Octopus = 0ctopus OR 0c70pu5
Octagon = 0ctagon OR 0c7490z
Occult = 0ccult OR 0ccu17

P

The letter P.
The sixteenth letter in the English modern alphabet.

It can be written as follows in C0D3:
P = 9

Examples of P in C0D3:

Penguin = 9enguin OR 93z9u1z
Pill = 9ill OR 9177
Popcorn = 9o9corn OR 909c02z

Q

The letter Q.
The seventeenth letter in the English modern alphabet.

It can be written as follows in C0D3:
Q = 9

Examples of Q in C0D3:

Quick = 9uick or 9u1ck
Quota = 9uota or 9u074
Qualify = 9ualify or 9u471fy

R

The letter R.
The eighteenth letter in the English modern alphabet.

It can be written as follows in C0D3:
R = 2

Examples of R in C0D3:

Row = 2ow OR 20m
Rat = 2at OR 247
Rump = 2ump or 2uw9

S

The letter S.
The nineteenth letter in the English modern alphabet.

It can be written as follows in C0D3:
S = 5

Examples of S in C0D3:

Sam = 5am OR 54w
Snake = 5nake OR 5z4k3
Silly = 5illy OR 5177y

T

The letter T.
The twentieth letter in the English modern alphabet.

It can be written as follows in C0D3:
T = 7

Examples of T in C0D3:

Thomas = 7homas OR 7h0w45
Tank = 7ank OR 74zk
Turnip = 7urnip OR 7u2z19

U

The letter U.
The fifth vowel and twenty first letter of the English modern alphabet.

In 1337 code no such code exists for masking the letter u. A usual letter U applies amongst other letters or code.

Examples of U in C0D3:

Utah = U7ah OR U74h
Unicorn = Uzicorn OR Uz1c02z
Umbrella = Uwbrella OR Uw823774

V

The letter V.
The twenty second letter in the English modern alphabet.

In 1337 code no such code exists for masking the letter v. A usual letter V applies amongst other letters or code.

Examples of V in C0D3:

Victory = V1ctory OR V1c702y
Vice = V1ce OR V1c3
Vehicle = V3hicle or V3h1c73

W

The letter W.
The twenty third letter of the English modern alphabet.

It can be written as follows in C0D3:
W = m

Examples of W in C0D3:

Water =Mater or M4732
Wonka = Monka or M0zk4
Went = Ment or M3z7

X

The letter X.
The twenty fourth letter in the English modern alphabet.

In 1337 code no such code exists for masking the letter x. A usual letter X applies amongst other letters or code.

Examples of X in C0D3:

X-ray = X-2ay OR X-24y
Xylophone = Xy1ophone OR Xy109h0z3
Xerox = X3rox or X320x

Y

The letter Y.
The twenty fifth letter in the English modern alphabet.

In 1337 code no such code exists for masking the letter y. A usual letter Y applies amongst other letters or code.

Examples of Y in C0D3:

Yellow = Y3llow OR y3770m
Yo-yo = Y0-yo OR Y0-y0
Yolk = Y0lk OR Y07k

Z

The letter Z.
The twenty sixth letter in the English modern alphabet.

It can be written as follows in C0D3:
Z = n

Examples of Z in C0D3:

Zerbra = N3bra OR N3824
Zoro = N0ro OR N020
Zelda = N3lda OR N37D4

Printed in the United States
By Bookmasters